HISTORIC PLACES *of the* UNITED KINGDOM

CHRISTIAN SITES

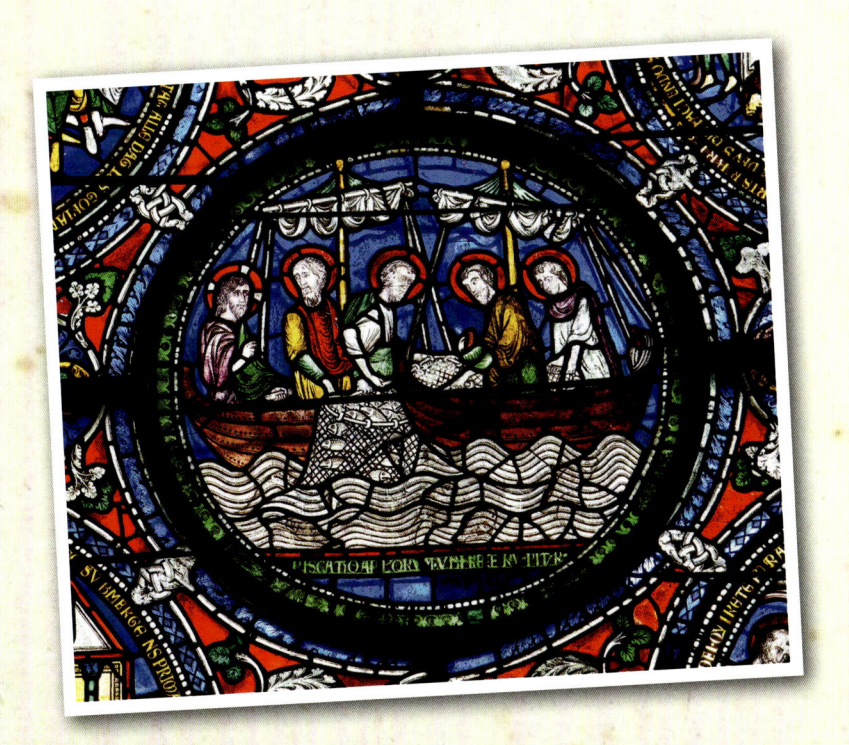

John Malam

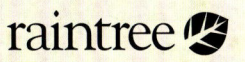

raintree
a Capstone company — publishers for children

Raintree is an imprint of Capstone Global Library Limited, a company incorporated in England and Wales having its registered office at 264 Banbury Road, Oxford, OX2 7DY – Registered company number: 6695582

www.raintree.co.uk

myorders@raintree.co.uk

Text © Capstone Global Library Limited 2018

The moral rights of the proprietor have been asserted.

All rights reserved. No part of this publication may be reproduced in any form or by any means (including photocopying or storing it in any medium by electronic means and whether or not transiently or incidentally to some other use of this publication) without the written permission of the copyright owner, except in accordance with the provisions of the Copyright, Designs and Patents Act 1988 or under the terms of a licence issued by the Copyright Licensing Agency, Saffron House, 6–10 Kirby Street, London, EC1N 8TS (www.cla.co.uk). Applications for the copyright owner's written permission should be addressed to the publisher.

Produced for Raintree by

White-Thomson Publishing Ltd
+44 (0)1273 477 216
www.wtpub.co.uk

Edited by Sonya Newland
Designed by Rocket Design (East Anglia) Ltd
Original illustrations © Capstone Global Library Ltd 2017
Illustrated by Ron Dixon
Production by Duncan Gilbert
Originated by Capstone Global Library Ltd
Printed and bound in China

ISBN 978 1 4747 5408 8
21 20 19 18 17
10 9 8 7 6 5 4 3 2 1

British Library Cataloguing in Publication Data
A full catalogue record for this book is available from the British Library.

Acknowledgements
We would like to thank the following for permission to reproduce photographs:
Alamy: geogphotos, 14, Granger Historical Picture Archive, 4, 5, Julie Woodhouse, 25, Tom Gardner, 18; Courtesy of the Portable Antiquities Scheme: 5 bottom (ID: NLM-A08783), 11 bottom (ID: PUBLIC364487); Shutterstock: Alastair Wallace, 32, Andrew Roland, 15, Christoph Lischetzki, 23, Claudio Divizia, 28, Dave Head, 16, Dmitry Naumov, 6, Gail Johnson, 19 bottom, 20, givi585, 17, Jeremy Alan Baxter, 27, jorisvo, 21, Michael Lazor, 13 bottom, Michael Warwick, 24, Pawel Kowalczyk, 8, Philip Bird LRPS CPAGB, 11 top, Platslee, 9, sofifoto, 22, Spumador, cover, Thoom, 12, Tupungato, 7, WDG Photo, 29, Yuri Turkov, 26; Wikimedia: 13 top, 19 top, Jastrow, 10.

We would like to thank Philip Parker for his help in the preparation of this book.

Every effort has been made to contact copyright holders of material reproduced in this book. Any omissions will be rectified in subsequent printings if notice is given to the publisher.

All the internet addresses (URLs) given in this book were valid at the time of going to press. However, due to the dynamic nature of the internet, some addresses may have changed, or sites may have changed or ceased to exist since publication. While the author and publisher regret any inconvenience this may cause readers, no responsibility for any such changes can be accepted by either the author or the publisher.

CONTENTS

In the beginning	4
St Martin's Church	6
Canterbury Cathedral	8
Holy island of Iona	12
St David's Cathedral	14
Lindisfarne Priory	16
Whitby Abbey	20
Westminster Abbey	22
Fountains Abbey	24
Coventry Cathedral	28
Timeline	29
Glossary	30
Find out more	31
Index	32

Some words are shown in bold, **like this**. You can find out what they mean by looking in the glossary.

IN THE BEGINNING

Just over 2,000 years ago, a new religion began. It was based on the teachings of Jesus Christ, and it became known as Christianity. Around 1,700 years ago, Christianity reached Britain.

Romans against Christians

Christianity began in Judea (present-day Israel) in the 1st century AD. At that time, Judea was part of the **Roman Empire**. Christianity slowly spread. By about AD 50, it had reached the city of Rome, the capital of the Roman Empire. At first, the Romans did not accept Christianity. They **persecuted** Christians for their beliefs.

chi-rho, the symbol for Christ

pomegranate, for eternal life

The oldest image of Jesus Christ found in Britain is this Roman **mosaic** from a **villa** at Hinton St Mary, Dorset. It was made in the early AD 300s.

Britain's first Christians

By the early AD 300s, Christianity had reached Britain. We know this because of some remarkable discoveries. For example, a Roman villa at Lullingstone, Kent, had a wall painting of Christians praying. Another villa, at Hinton St Mary, Dorset, had a mosaic showing the head of Christ surrounded by Christian symbols.

Christian cross appearing to Emperor Constantine

Emperor Constantine

DIG DEEPER

** PERSECUTION ENDS **

In AD 312, the Roman **emperor** Constantine (AD 272–337) had a vision before a battle in Rome. He believed he saw a Christian cross in the sky. He took this as a sign that the Christian god was on his side. Constantine won the battle. After that, he allowed Christianity in the Roman Empire.

This coin was made around AD 352. It shows Emperor Magnentius (AD 303–353). On the back is the chi-rho symbol.

chi-rho symbol

ST MARTIN'S CHURCH

Some of the oldest buildings still in use in Britain are Christian places. They are churches where Christians have gathered to **worship** for hundreds of years. Some are more than 1,000 years old.

Queen Bertha's chapel

St Martin's, Canterbury, is said to be the oldest church in Britain still in use as a church. In the AD 580s, King Ethelbert of Kent (AD 560–616) married Princess Bertha from France. He was **pagan** and she was Christian. Ethelbert gave Bertha an old Roman building at Canterbury to use as a **chapel**.

ST MARTIN'S CHURCH

WHAT: St Martin's Church
WHERE: Canterbury, Kent
WHEN: about AD 597

St Martin's Church has changed a lot since it began as the chapel of Queen Bertha.

Roman bricks, AD 300s

Saxon addition, AD 600s

bell tower, 1300s

Pagans into Christians

In AD 597, a group of about 40 **monks**, led by Augustine, came to Britain. They wanted to convert pagans to Christianity. Augustine used Bertha's chapel as his base. He rebuilt it as a church. It was named St Martin's after a saint from Bertha's home town. Soon after Augustine arrived in Canterbury, Ethelbert converted to Christianity.

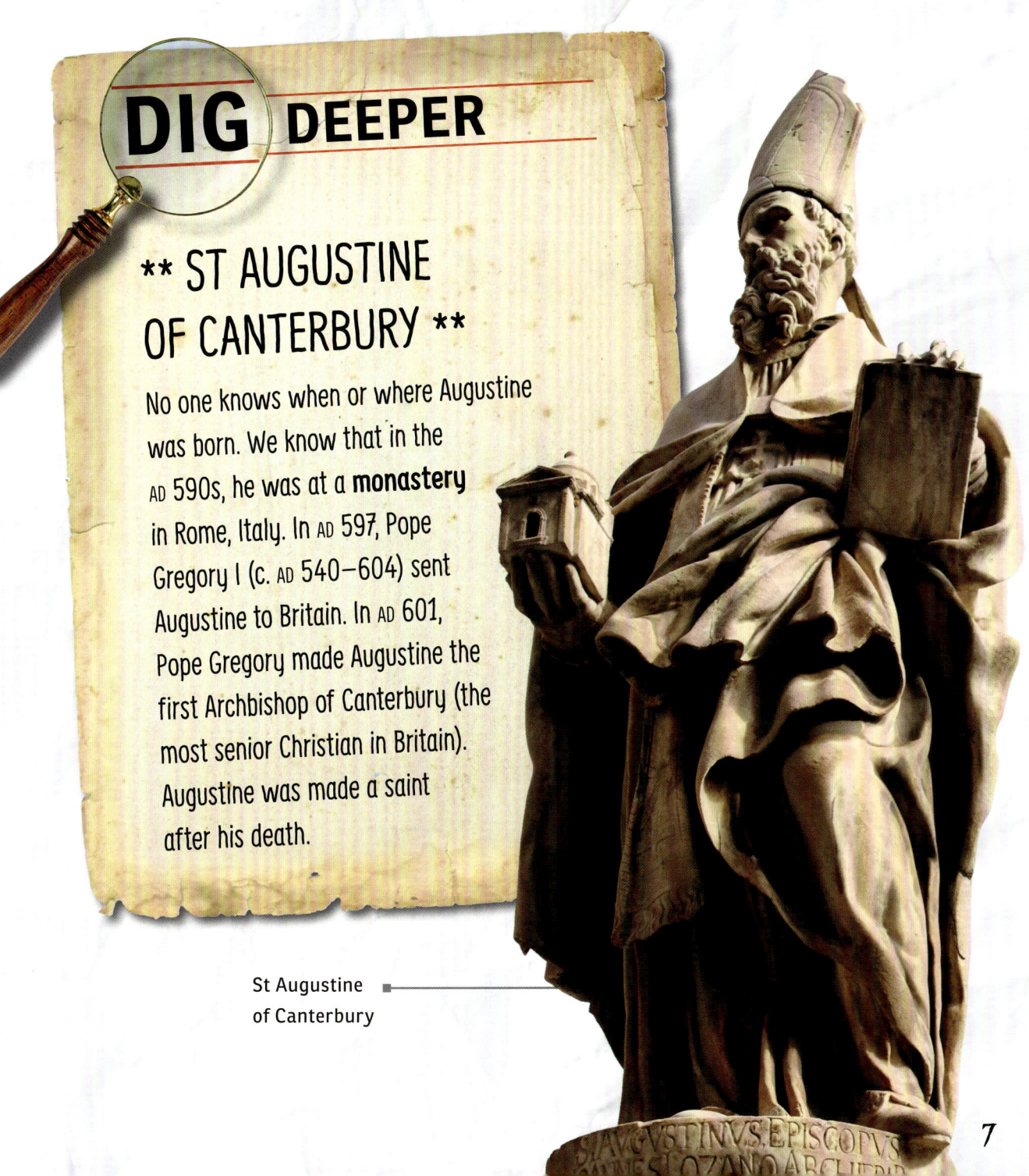

DIG DEEPER

** ST AUGUSTINE OF CANTERBURY **

No one knows when or where Augustine was born. We know that in the AD 590s, he was at a **monastery** in Rome, Italy. In AD 597, Pope Gregory I (c. AD 540–604) sent Augustine to Britain. In AD 601, Pope Gregory made Augustine the first Archbishop of Canterbury (the most senior Christian in Britain). Augustine was made a saint after his death.

St Augustine of Canterbury

CANTERBURY CATHEDRAL

Canterbury Cathedral is one of the most important cathedrals in Britain. It is known by Christians throughout the world.

Christian centre

When Augustine came to Britain in AD 597, he intended to make his headquarters in London. But Ethelbert and Bertha of Kent welcomed him so warmly that he changed his mind and stayed in Canterbury. He built a cathedral there. Canterbury is regarded as the birthplace of Christianity in England.

CANTERBURY CATHEDRAL

WHAT: Canterbury Cathedral
WHERE: Canterbury, Kent
WHEN: founded AD 597

bell tower

Canterbury Cathedral was built from stone that was brought over from France.

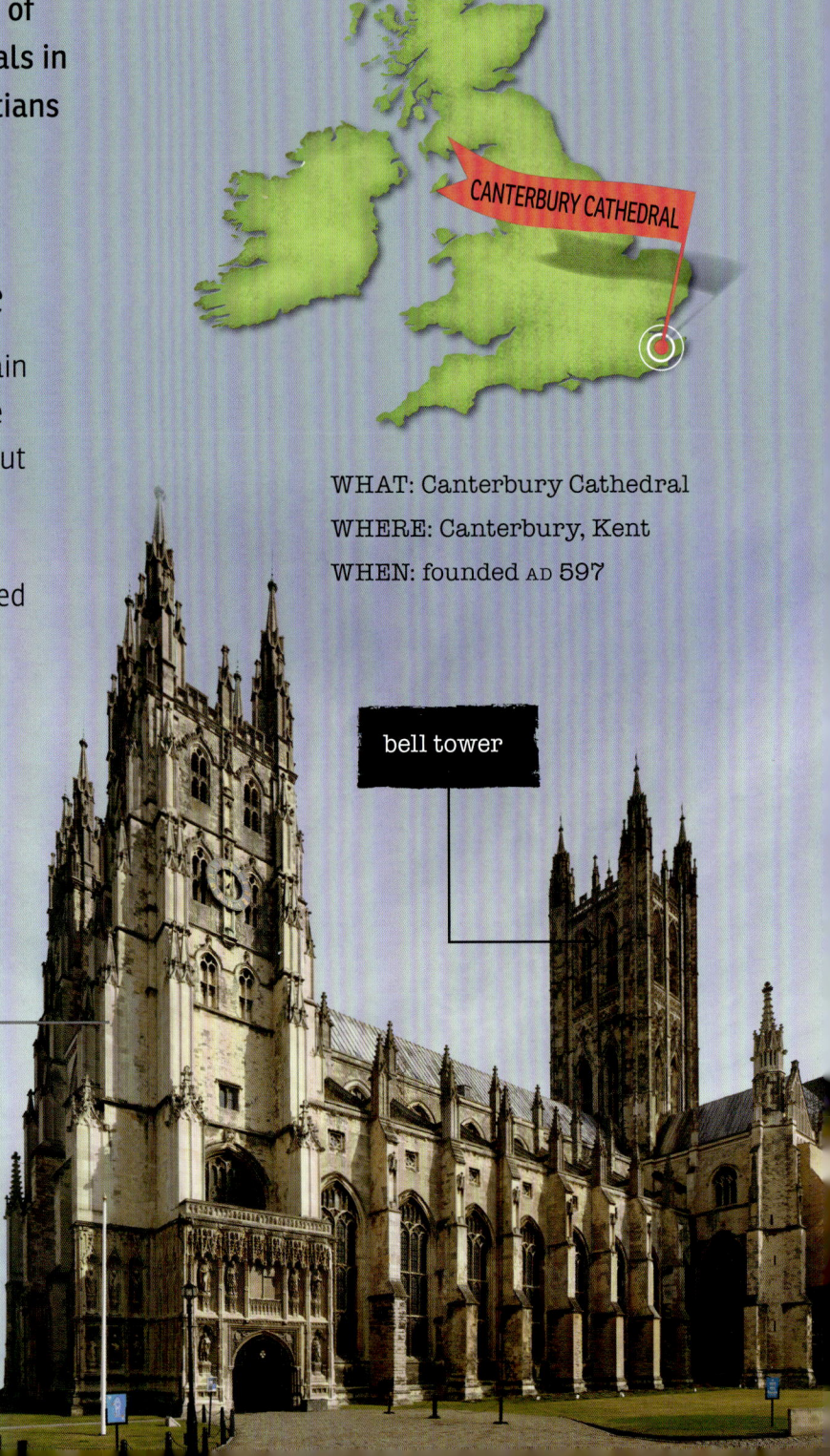

Fire and earthquake

Canterbury Cathedral has been rebuilt and added to over the centuries. Augustine's cathedral was destroyed by fire in 1067. A grander cathedral was begun in 1070, but part of that burned down in 1174. It was rebuilt and new parts were added. An earthquake shook the cathedral in 1382 and the bells fell to the ground. A bell tower was added in about 1500, making the cathedral building we see today.

DIG DEEPER

** WHAT IS A CATHEDRAL? **

A cathedral is the main church of a **diocese**, an area under the control of a **bishop**. A cathedral is often described as the "seat of a bishop". This is because the bishop has a special chair, or throne, in the cathedral. The Latin word for chair is *cathedra*, which is where the word *cathedral* comes from.

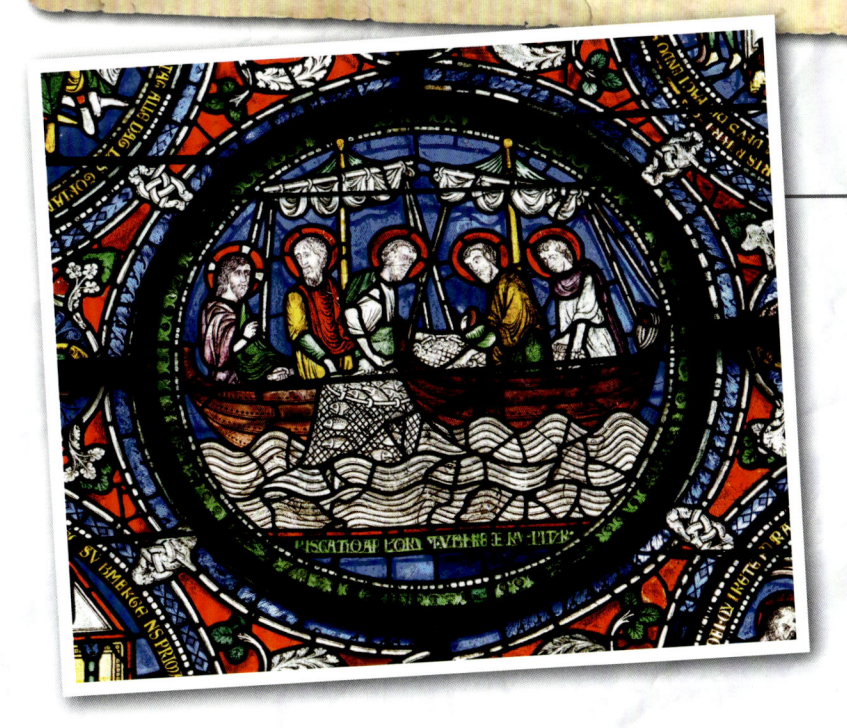

Some of Britain's oldest stained glass windows are at Canterbury Cathedral. Many were made about 800 years ago.

Murder in the cathedral

On 29 December 1170, four knights entered Canterbury Cathedral. They were looking for Archbishop Thomas Becket (1118–1170). They found him at the altar, and killed him with their swords. The knights believed they were following the orders of King Henry II (1133–1189). The king and the archbishop had quarrelled. In a temper, Henry is supposed to have said: "Will no one rid me of this turbulent priest?" The knights took the king at his word and killed Becket.

A box showing Becket's murder. It was made to hold some of his hair or a piece of bone (known as relics).

Becoming a saint

Becket was buried inside the cathedral. Before long, Christians were calling him a **martyr**. In 1173, Pope Alexander III (1100–1181) made Becket a saint – St Thomas of Canterbury. People said that **miracles** happened at his tomb. **Pilgrims** visited the tomb to ask for God's help.

■ Becket's tomb was destroyed in 1540, on the orders of King Henry VIII. Today, a candle burns where his tomb once stood.

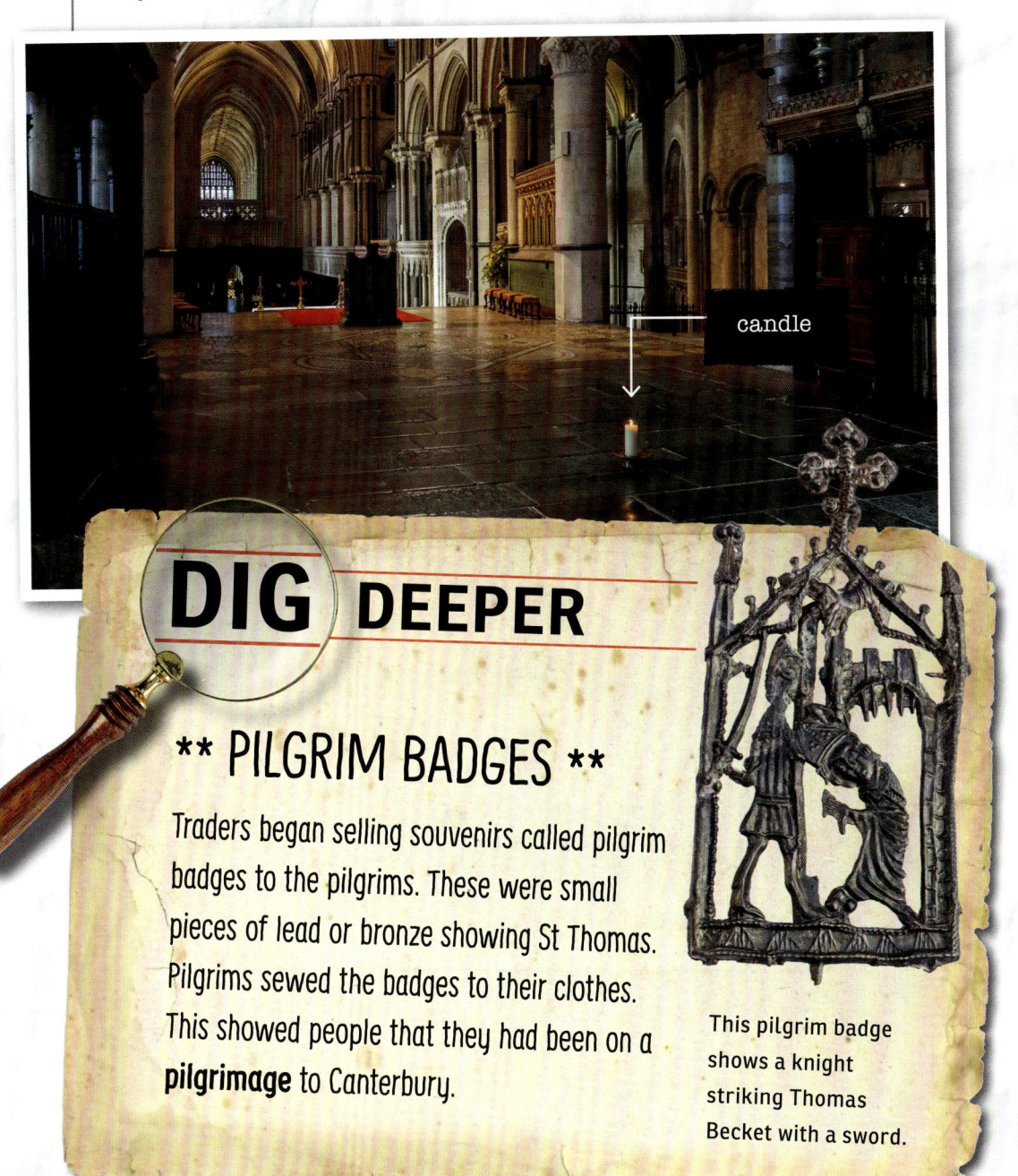

candle

DIG DEEPER

** PILGRIM BADGES **

Traders began selling souvenirs called pilgrim badges to the pilgrims. These were small pieces of lead or bronze showing St Thomas. Pilgrims sewed the badges to their clothes. This showed people that they had been on a **pilgrimage** to Canterbury.

This pilgrim badge shows a knight striking Thomas Becket with a sword.

HOLY ISLAND OF IONA

Iona is one of many islands off the west coast of Scotland. A **monk** from Ireland built a **monastery** there. Christian **missionaries** travelled from Iona to mainland Scotland and northern England.

IONA ABBEY

WHAT: Iona **Abbey**
WHERE: Iona, Scotland
WHEN: founded AD 563

Monks on a mission

In AD 563, a group of 12 monks led by St Columba (AD 521–597) crossed the sea from Ireland to Scotland. A Scottish king gave St Columba the island of Iona. This became the base for his mission to convert the **pagans** of Scotland to Christianity. Iona is regarded as the birthplace of Christianity in Scotland.

This stained glass window shows St Columba setting off on his mission to Scotland.

DIG DEEPER

** THE BOOK OF KELLS **

The Book of Kells is one of the greatest works of early Christian art. Written in Latin in about AD 800, it is thought to have been created by the monks of Iona. It contains the **Gospels** of Matthew, Mark, Luke and John. They are richly decorated with colourful pictures.

This page from the Book of Kells shows Mary and the infant Jesus.

Place of pilgrimage

Nothing remains of St Columba's monastery. However, it can be imagined as a small wooden church with rooms where monks lived and prayed. **Pilgrims** came to **worship** there, but not all visitors came in peace. In AD 849, **Viking raiders** forced the monks to flee to Kells in Ireland. Despite this, Iona has remained a sacred place.

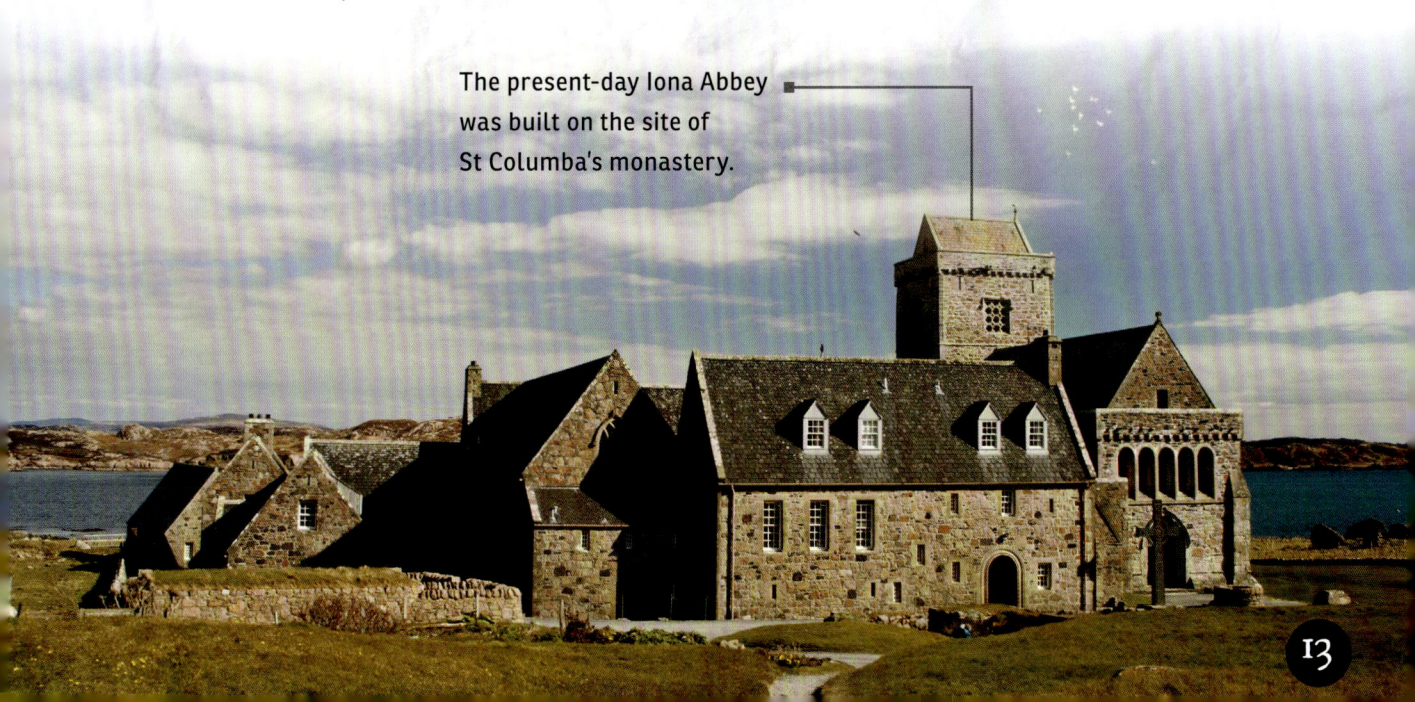

The present-day Iona Abbey was built on the site of St Columba's monastery.

ST DAVID'S CATHEDRAL

About 1,500 years ago, a **monastery** was built at St Davids, South Wales. It grew into a cathedral where the bones of a saint were kept. Today, St Davids is the Christian capital of Wales.

St David, patron saint of Wales

St David was born in South Wales in about AD 500. He became a **monk**, and it was said that he could perform **miracles**. In about AD 550, David founded a monastery at Menevia (an old name for the city of St Davids). He died there in AD 589.

WHAT: St David's Cathedral
WHERE: St Davids, Pembrokeshire, Wales
WHEN: about AD 550

A legend says this well at St Davids appeared on the day St David was born. Its water was thought to have healing powers.

From monastery to cathedral

Stories about David's miracles were told long after his death. In 1120, Pope Calixtus II (1065–1124) made him a saint. By then, a cathedral had been built on the site of David's monastery. Inside was a **shrine**, where St David's bones were kept. Pope Calixtus said the shrine was extremely important. Making two **pilgrimages** to it was the same as one pilgrimage to Rome (the world centre of Christianity). Three visits were as good as one visit to Jerusalem (where Jesus Christ died and was buried).

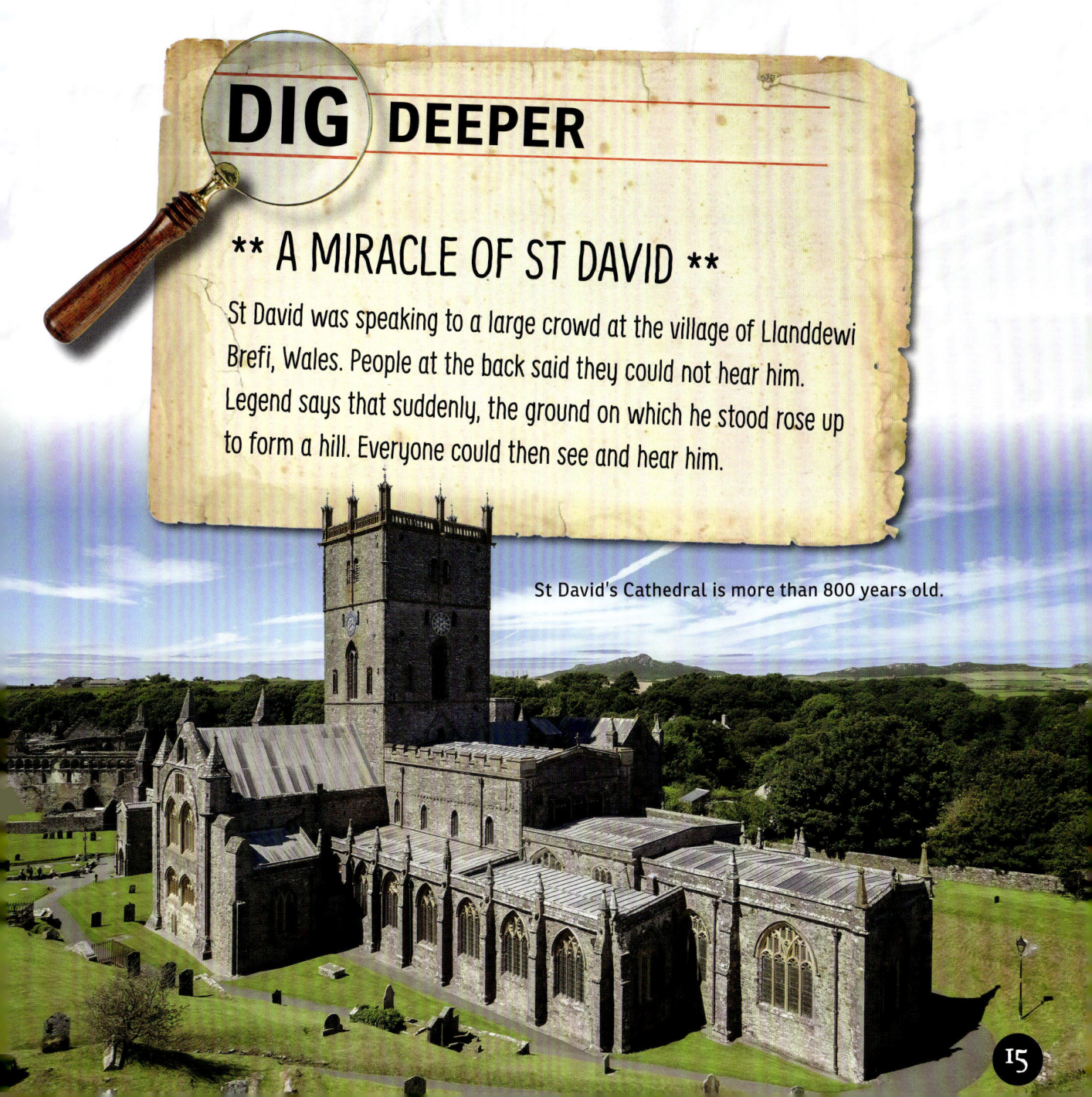

DIG DEEPER

** A MIRACLE OF ST DAVID **

St David was speaking to a large crowd at the village of Llanddewi Brefi, Wales. People at the back said they could not hear him. Legend says that suddenly, the ground on which he stood rose up to form a hill. Everyone could then see and hear him.

St David's Cathedral is more than 800 years old.

LINDISFARNE PRIORY

Off the coast of Northumberland in northeastern England is a tiny island called Lindisfarne, or Holy Island. Twice a day, when the sea is out, people can walk or drive across to the island. At high tide, it is cut off by the sea.

Peaceful place

Many early Christian sites in Britain are remote and hard to reach. Christians chose these places because they were far away from towns and the troubles of the world. People could follow a Christian lifestyle there. They could pray, study the Bible and feel close to God. The island of Lindisfarne is one of these places.

WHAT: Lindisfarne Priory
WHERE: Lindisfarne, Northumberland
WHEN: AD 635

At high tide Lindisfarne is an island surrounded by the sea.

Building a monastery

In AD 635, a group of **monks** from the **monastery** on Iona, Scotland (see page 12), moved to Lindisfarne. The island was given to them by King Oswald of Northumbria (AD 604–642). The monks were led by an Irish monk named Aidan. Oswald wanted Aidan to set up a Christian community on Lindisfarne. Soon after they arrived, they began to build a priory (a small monastery).

DIG DEEPER

** ST CUTHBERT AT LINDISFARNE **

In the AD 670s, a monk called Cuthbert joined the monastery at Lindisfarne. He became the head monk, and it was said that he had healing powers. Cuthbert died in AD 687. Eleven years later, the monks discovered that his body had not rotted away as dead bodies normally do. Lindisfarne became a place of **pilgrimage. Miracles** were said to happen at St Cuthbert's **shrine**.

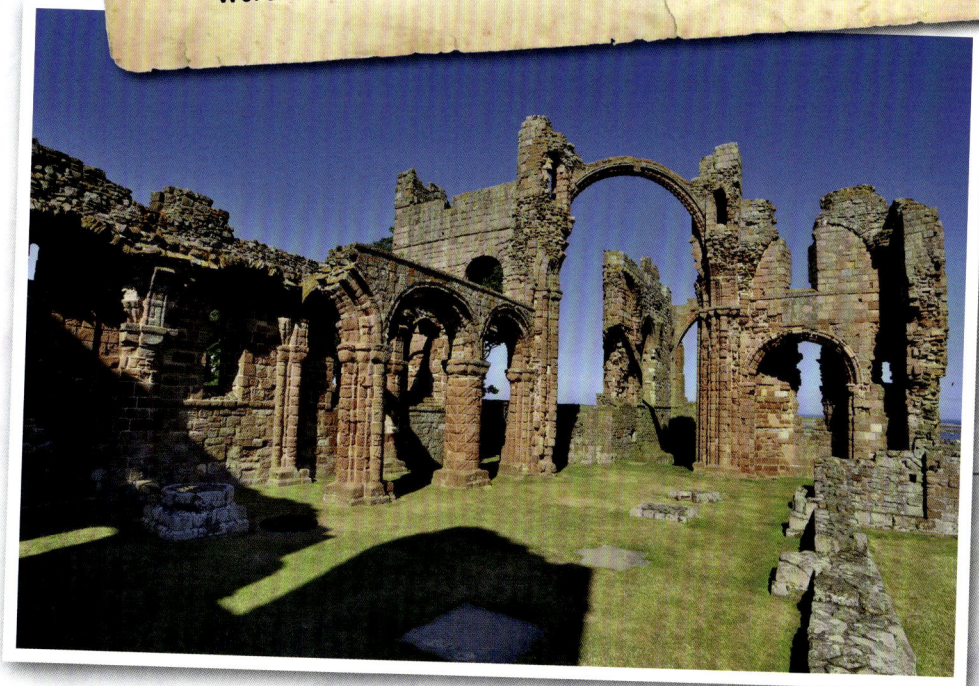

the ruins of Lindisfarne Priory

Viking attack!

The monks on Lindisfarne enjoyed the peace of their island home. But in AD 793, that peace was shattered by a band of **Viking raiders**. The Vikings murdered some of the monks. They set fire to buildings and stole treasures from the monastery. This marked the start of a long period of Viking raids against Britain.

St Cuthbert at Durham

In AD 875, the Vikings returned and the monks fled. They took their most precious possession – the body of St Cuthbert – with them. For years, the monks searched for a new home. Eventually they settled in Durham, in northeastern England. St Cuthbert's body was placed inside a small church there. In 1093, Durham Cathedral was built on the site of the church. A grand shrine was made for the saint's body, and this shrine became a place of pilgrimage.

This sculpture from St Mary's Church on Lindisfarne shows the monks carrying away St Cuthbert's body.

DIG DEEPER

** THE LINDISFARNE GOSPELS **

In the early AD 700s, monks at Lindisfarne monastery made a beautiful handwritten book. Known as the Lindisfarne Gospels, it is the **Gospels** of Matthew, Mark, Luke and John. It was written on 258 pages of vellum (calf skin). Historians think it was made around the time Cuthbert became a saint.

the first page of the Gospel of Luke, from the Lindisfarne Gospels

Work on Durham Cathedral began in 1093 to house the remains of St Cuthbert.

WHITBY ABBEY

On a cliff above Whitby, North Yorkshire, are the ruins of an **abbey**. It was built on the site of a **monastery**, where a meeting decided the date of Easter.

Centre of teaching

Whitby Abbey was founded in AD 657 by a nun called Hilda. She became its first **abbess**. It grew into an important centre for Christian teaching in northern Britain. Legends say at the very moment Hilda died, in AD 680, the bells at a nearby monastery rang out by themselves. They also say that angels were seen carrying her up to heaven. In time, she became St Hilda of Whitby.

WHITBY ABBEY

WHAT: Whitby Abbey
WHERE: Whitby, North Yorkshire
WHEN: AD 657

the ruins of Whitby Abbey

An important meeting

In AD 664, Whitby monastery was chosen as the place to hold a meeting of leading Christians called a **synod**. The meeting was to decide the date of Easter. This was the cause of an argument between two groups of Christians who had different ways of working out the date. At the Synod of Whitby, it was decided that Christians in Britain would celebrate Easter on the same day as Christians in Rome and elsewhere.

DIG DEEPER

** CLOSE SHAVE **

British **monks** had two different hairstyles. Some shaved the tops of their heads while others shaved their heads from ear to ear. The Synod of Whitby decided that monks in Britain should shave the tops of their heads.

A monk shaved his head to show he was following a holy lifestyle.

WESTMINSTER ABBEY

Westminster **Abbey** is one of the best-known Christian sites in Britain. Kings and queens have been crowned there. They have also been married in the abbey, and many are buried there.

Crowning glory

In the 1040s, King Edward the Confessor (1003–1066) began building a large church in London, near the River Thames. It became known as Westminster Abbey. Edward died in January 1066, just a few days after the opening ceremony. He was the first person to be buried at the abbey. On Christmas Day that year, the abbey was used for its first known coronation when William the Conqueror was crowned king.

WHAT: Westminster Abbey
WHERE: London
WHEN: founded AD 1040s

DIG DEEPER

** WATER SPITTERS **

Poking out along the roof of Westminster Abbey are strange-looking creatures carved in stone. These **gargoyles** all have wide-open mouths. In a storm, water gushes from their mouths and away from the walls of the building.

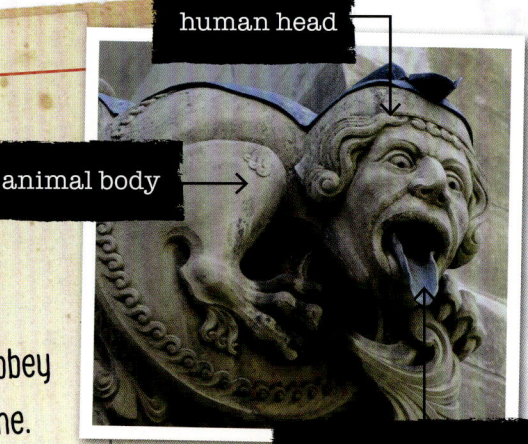

a gargoyle at Westminster Abbey

- human head
- animal body
- rainwater spout

Gothic style

In the early 1200s, a new style of building known as **Gothic** came into fashion. It was particularly popular for churches and cathedrals. In the 1240s, King Henry III (1207–1272) began to rebuild Westminster Abbey in the Gothic style. He included pointed arches, **buttresses** and **pinnacles**. This is the great building we see today.

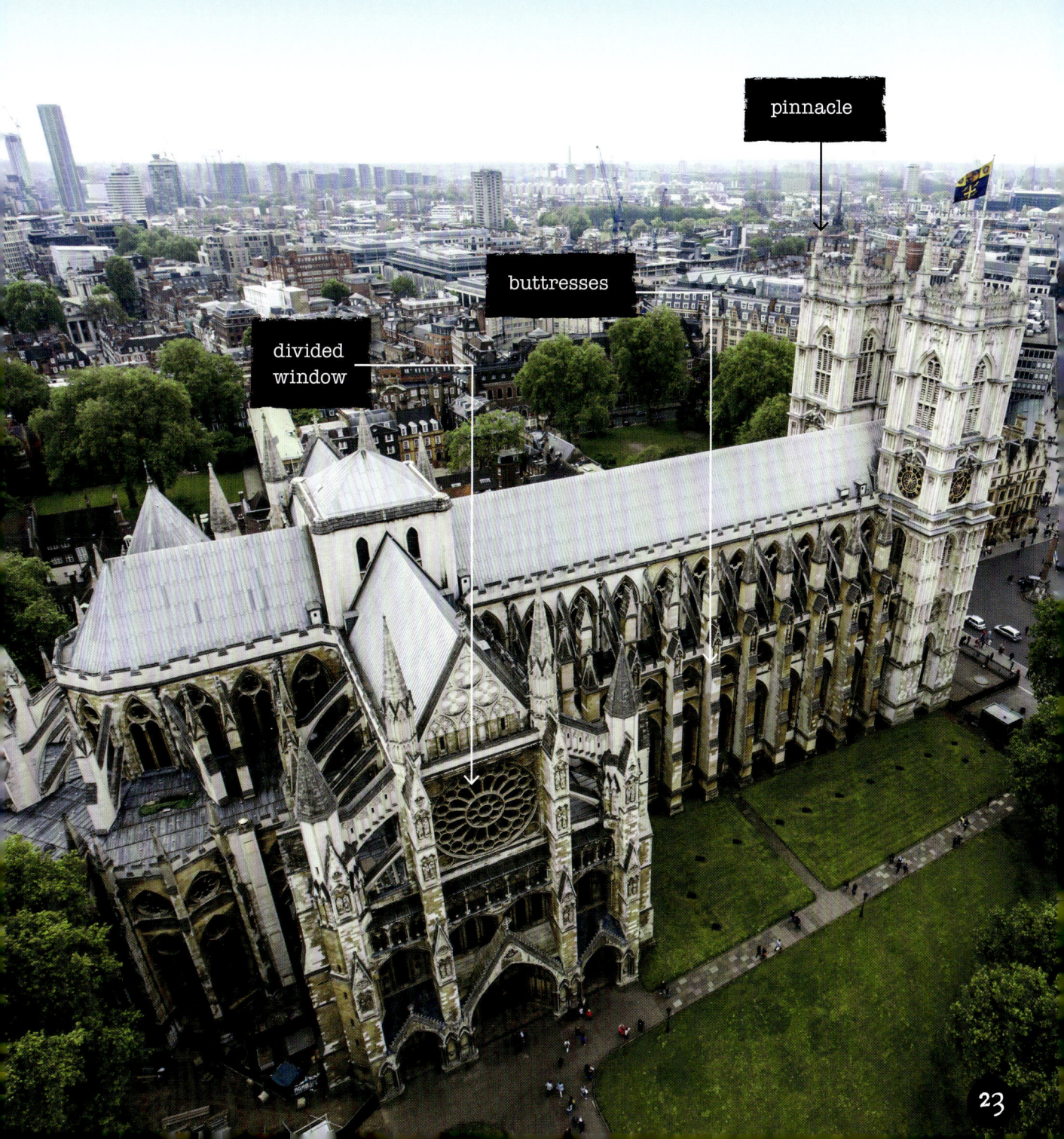

pinnacle

buttresses

divided window

FOUNTAINS ABBEY

We think of **monks** as people who live simple lives without many possessions. So how did many **abbeys** become rich and powerful? And why did so many of them fall into ruin? The story of Fountains Abbey gives us the answers.

Worker monks

In 1132, a group of Benedictine monks left St Mary's Abbey in York. They wanted to lead a stricter lifestyle, so they joined the Cistercian order of monks. They were given land on which to build a **monastery**. They named it Fountains Abbey after the **springs** at the site. The Cistercian monks introduced the system of unpaid worker monks, known as **lay brothers**.

WHAT: Fountains Abbey, monastery
WHERE: near Ripon, North Yorkshire
WHEN: 1132

Fountains Abbey is the largest ruined monastery in Britain.

A wealthy abbey

By the end of the 1200s, Fountains Abbey owned a large amount of land. The abbey was home to about 1,200 monks. Four hundred of these monks spent their days in prayer. There were also 800 worker monks who ran the abbey's farms, raised cattle, and traded wool and lead. It was one of the richest abbeys in Britain.

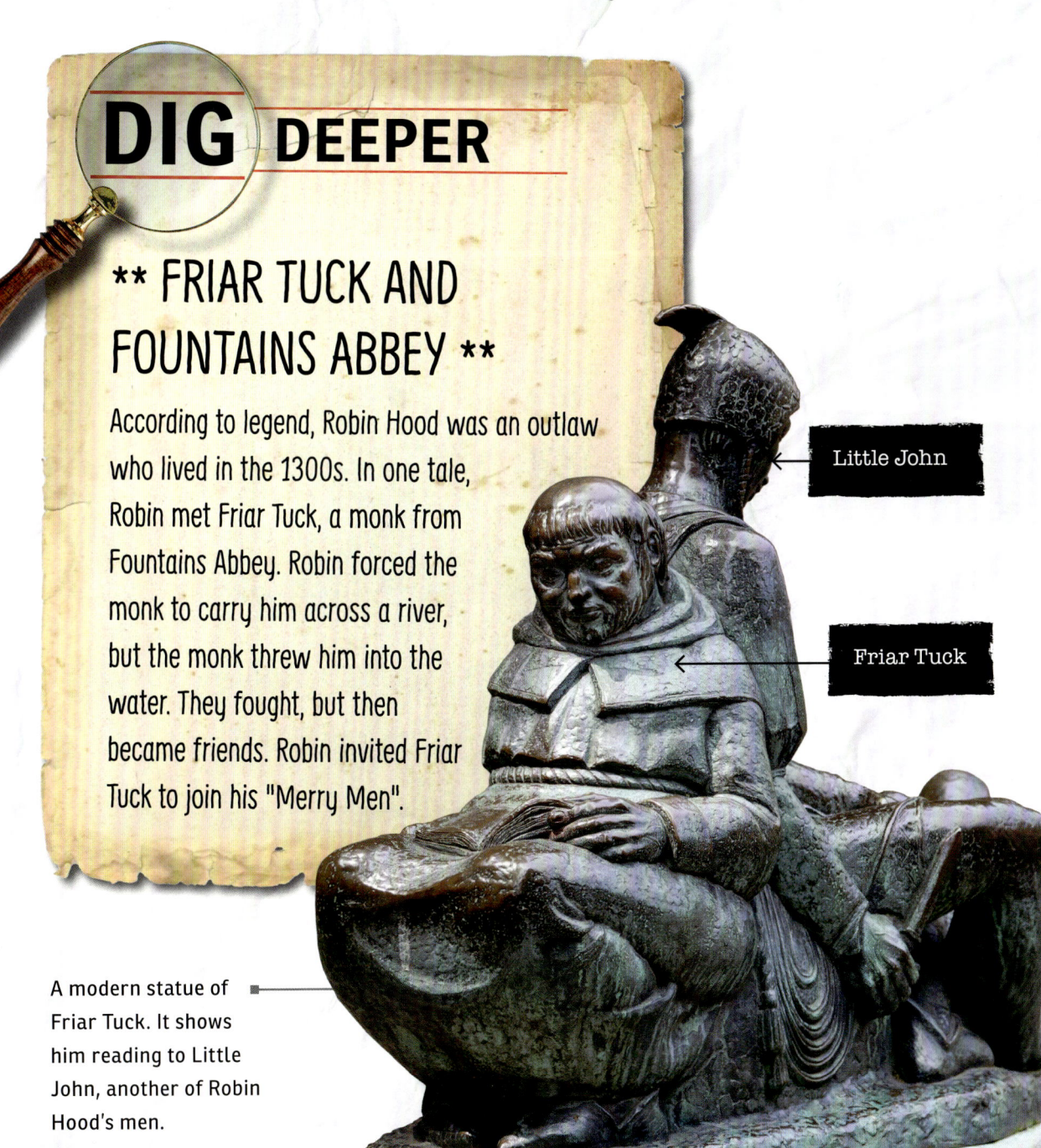

DIG DEEPER

** FRIAR TUCK AND FOUNTAINS ABBEY **

According to legend, Robin Hood was an outlaw who lived in the 1300s. In one tale, Robin met Friar Tuck, a monk from Fountains Abbey. Robin forced the monk to carry him across a river, but the monk threw him into the water. They fought, but then became friends. Robin invited Friar Tuck to join his "Merry Men".

Little John

Friar Tuck

A modern statue of Friar Tuck. It shows him reading to Little John, another of Robin Hood's men.

The dissolution of the monasteries

Henry VIII (1491–1547) became king in 1509. At the time, there were hundreds of monasteries, abbeys and other religious buildings in England. They were as much a part of the landscape as castles, cathedrals and churches. But time was running out for the monks and nuns. Henry quarrelled with the Pope and declared himself head of the Church in England. Henry discovered that many monasteries were hugely rich and dishonest places. He began closing them down. The king took their land and possessions for himself.

King Henry VIII (reigned 1509–1547), ordered many monasteries to be closed down.

End of Fountains Abbey

In 1536, William Thirsk, the **abbot** of Fountains Abbey, joined a protest against Henry's actions. Thirsk was arrested, and the following year he was hanged. Other abbots who had joined the protest were also executed. In 1539, Fountains Abbey was forced to close. The monks left. Their 2,356 cattle, 1,326 sheep, 86 horses, 79 pigs and stores of grain were sold to the Lord Mayor of London. The buildings gradually fell into ruin.

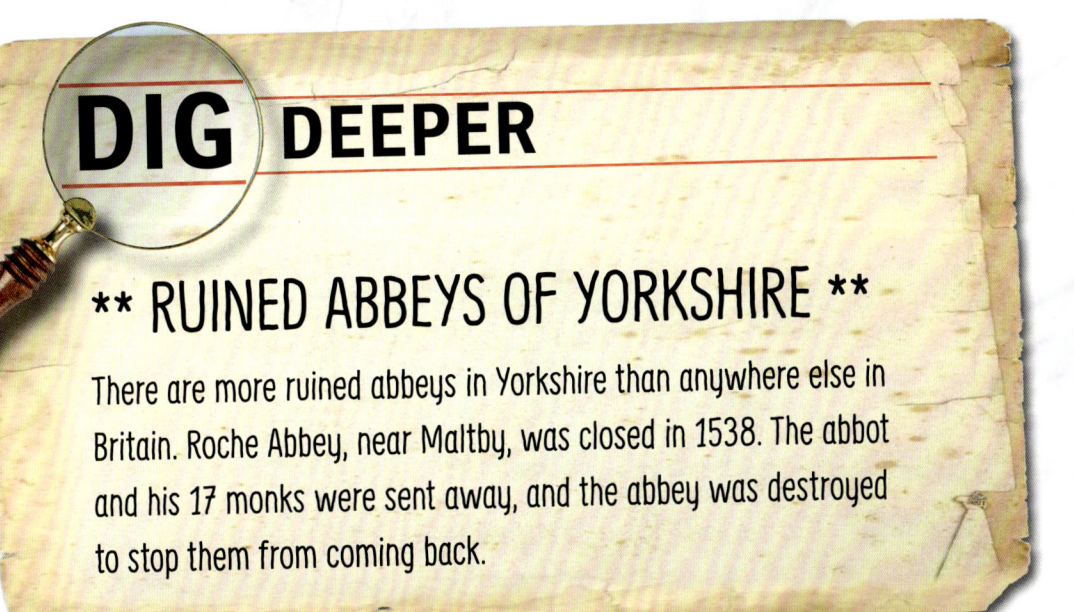

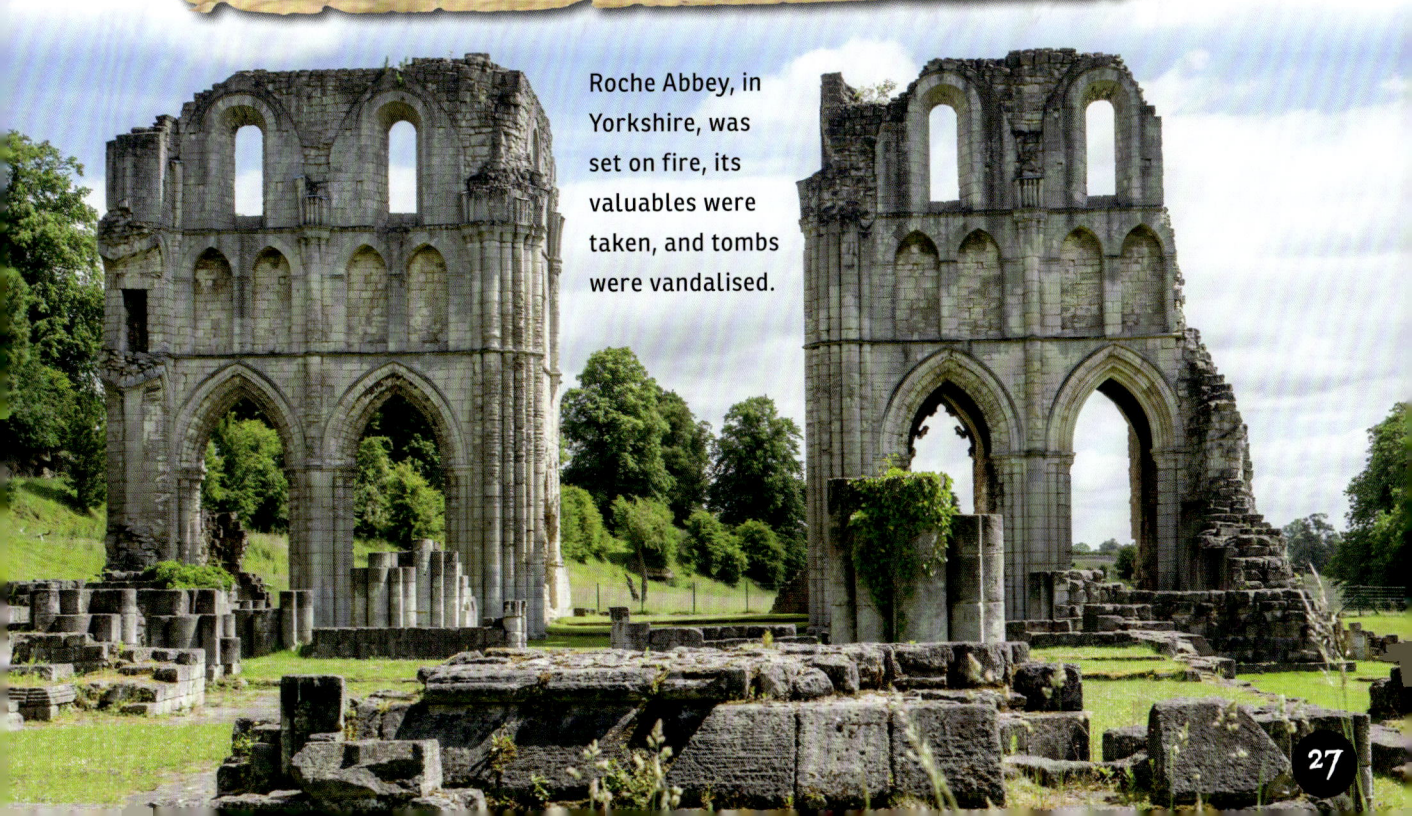

DIG DEEPER

** RUINED ABBEYS OF YORKSHIRE **

There are more ruined abbeys in Yorkshire than anywhere else in Britain. Roche Abbey, near Maltby, was closed in 1538. The abbot and his 17 monks were sent away, and the abbey was destroyed to stop them from coming back.

Roche Abbey, in Yorkshire, was set on fire, its valuables were taken, and tombs were vandalised.

COVENTRY CATHEDRAL

Not all Christian sites in Britain are old. It might seem that the church in your town has always been there, but there are many modern Christian buildings. Coventry Cathedral is one example.

A tale of two cathedrals

On the night of 14 November 1940, German warplanes dropped hundreds of bombs on the city of Coventry. World War II (1939–1945) was raging, and Coventry's factories made weapons. This made the city a target. The bombing raid reduced most of the city centre to rubble. The cathedral, which had stood there since the 1300s, was destroyed. After the war, a new cathedral was built next to the ruins of the old one. It was built in a modern style and was decorated with tapestries, sculptures and stained glass.

COVENTRY CATHEDRAL

WHAT: Coventry Cathedral
WHERE: Coventry, West Midlands
WHEN: 1300s and 1962

Coventry's modern cathedral, built in the 1960s, joins onto the ruins of the ancient one.

Timeline

AD 33	Death of Jesus Christ and the beginning of Christianity.
AD 50	Christianity reaches the city of Rome.
AD 300s	Christianity is practised by some people living in Roman Britain.
AD 312	Emperor Constantine converts to Christianity. Christians are allowed to follow their faith in the Roman Empire.
AD 550	St David founds a monastery at St Davids, Wales.
AD 563	St Columba begins his missionary work in Scotland.
AD 597	St Augustine begins his missionary work in England.
AD 635	St Aidan establishes the monastery of Lindisfarne, Northumbria.
AD 664	The Synod of Whitby is held, which decides the date of Easter.
AD 700s	The Lindisfarne Gospels are written.
AD 800s	The Book of Kells is written.
1065	Westminster Abbey opens in London.
1170	Thomas Becket is murdered in Canterbury Cathedral.
1526	The Bible is printed in English rather than Latin for the first time.
1536–1540	King Henry VIII closes monasteries in England.

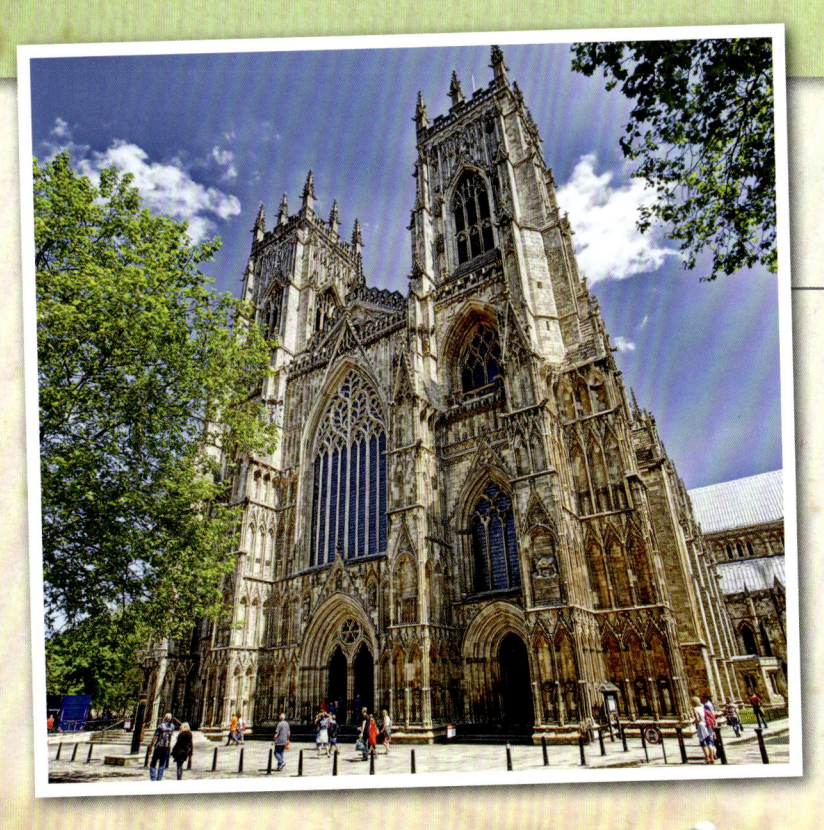

York Minster, in York, is one of Britain's finest cathedrals. About 600,000 people visit it every year. Only Westminster Abbey and Canterbury Cathedral have more visitors.

Glossary

abbess woman who is the head of an abbey of nuns

abbey building where monks or nuns live and work

abbot monk in charge of a monastery

bishop church leader in charge of a city or area

buttress support built against a wall to strengthen a building

chapel small church or a section in a larger church

chi-rho Christian symbol from the letters X (chi) and P (rho) – the first two letters of Christ's name in the Greek alphabet

diocese area containing a number of churches under the authority of a bishop

emperor male ruler of a country or group of countries

gargoyle make-believe creature made of stone

gospel one of the first four books of the New Testament of the Bible telling of the life, death and teachings of Jesus Christ

Gothic style of building popular in western Europe between the 1100s and 1500s

lay brother man who lives in a monastery and does its day-to-day work

martyr person who is killed because of his or her religious beliefs

miracle something amazing that is said to be the work of God

monastery group of buildings where monks live and work

monk man who lives in a religious community and promises to devote his life to his religion

mosaic picture made of tiny pieces of stone, glass or tile

pagan person who worships many gods instead of just one

persecute punish or treat badly for one's beliefs

pilgrim person who travels to a holy place for religious reasons

pilgrimage journey to a holy place for religious reasons

pinnacle slender tower generally coming to a point at the top

raider person who launches a sudden, surprise attack on a place

Roman Empire lands across Europe, North Africa and the Middle East that were under Roman control

shrine holy place, usually connected with a person or a miracle

spring place where water rises to the surface from an underground source

synod meeting of religious leaders

Vikings Scandinavian warriors who explored and invaded other parts of Europe and North America between the 8th and 11th centuries

villa large, fancy house, especially one in the country

worship to give praise or respect to God

Find out more

BOOKS
All About Henry VIII (Fusion: History), Anna Claybourne (Raintree, 2014)

The Book of Saints, Paul Harrison (Wayland, 2017)

Religion and Saints (Discover the Anglo-Saxons), Moira Butterfield (Franklin Watts, 2014)

Westminster Abbey (Crypts, Tombs, and Secret Rooms), Enzo George (Gareth Stevens Publishing, 2017)

WEBSITES
www.bbc.co.uk/northyorkshire/content/articles/2008/11/12/abbey_history_feature.shtml
Check out this article to learn all about this history of Fountains Abbey.

www.canterbury-cathedral.org/heritage/history/cathedral-history-in-a-nutshell/
Visit this website to learn more about the history of Canterbury Cathedral.

www.english-heritage.org.uk/visit/places/lindisfarne-priory/history/
Find out more about Lindisfarne Priory.

www.historic-uk.com/HistoryUK/HistoryofScotland/St-Columba-the-Isle-of-Iona/
Discover more about St Columba and the Holy Island of Iona at the Historic UK website.

http://kids.britannica.com/kids/article/Westminster-Abbey/476337
Want to learn more about Westminster Abbey? Check out Britannica Kids article.

PLACES TO VISIT
Canterbury Cathedral
Canterbury, Kent, CT1 2EH

Coventry Cathedral
Coventry, West Midlands, CV1 5AB

Durham Cathedral
Durham, DH1 3EH

Fountains Abbey
near Ripon, North Yorkshire, HG4 3DY

Iona Abbey
Isle of Iona, Scotland, PA76 6SQ

Lindisfarne Priory
Holy Island, near Berwick-upon-Tweed, Northumberland, TD15 2RX

St David's Cathedral
St Davids, Wales, SA62 6RD

Westminster Abbey
London, SW1P 3PA

Whitby Abbey
Whitby, North Yorkshire, YO22 4JT

Index

abbeys 12, 13, 20–21, 22–23, 24–27, 29
Aidan, St 17, 29
Alexander III, Pope 11
Archbishop of Canterbury 7, 10
Augustine, St 7, 8, 9, 29

Becket, Thomas 10–11, 29
bells 9, 20
bell towers 9
Bertha, Queen 6, 7, 8
Bible, the 16, 29
Book of Kells 13, 29

Calixtus II, Pope 15
Canterbury 6, 7, 8, 9, 11
Canterbury Cathedral 8–11, 29
cathedrals 8–11, 14–15, 18, 19, 23, 26, 28, 29
chi-rho symbol 4, 5
Christian symbols 4, 5
churches 6–7, 9, 13, 18, 22, 23, 26, 28
coins 5
Columba, St 12, 13, 29
Constantine, Emperor 5, 29
Coventry Cathedral 28
Cuthbert, St 17, 18, 19

David, St 14, 15, 29
Durham Cathedral 18, 19

earthquakes 9
Easter 20, 21, 29
Edward the Confessor 22
Ethelbert, King 6, 7, 8

fires 9, 18, 27
Fountains Abbey 24–27
Friar Tuck 25

gargoyles 22
Gospels 13, 19, 29
Gothic style 23
Gregory I, Pope 7

Henry II, King 10
Henry III, King 23
Henry VIII, King 11, 26, 29
Hilda of Whitby, St 20
Hinton St Mary, Dorset 4, 5

Iona 12–13, 17
Ireland 12, 13

Jerusalem 15
Jesus Christ 4, 5, 15, 29
Judea (Israel) 4

lay brothers 24, 25
Lindisfarne (Holy Island) 16–19, 29
Lindisfarne Gospels 19, 29
London 8, 22, 27, 29
Lullingstone, Kent 5

Magnentius, Emperor 5
miracles 11, 14, 15, 17
missionaries 12, 29
monasteries 7, 12, 13, 14, 15, 17, 18, 19, 20, 21, 24, 26, 29
monks 7, 12, 13, 14, 17, 18, 19, 21, 24, 25, 26, 27
mosaics 4, 5

nuns 20, 26

Oswald, King 17

pagans 6, 7, 12
persecution 4, 5
pilgrim badges 11
pilgrimages 11, 13, 15, 17, 18
pilgrims 11, 13

Liverpool Cathedral is the largest cathedral in Britain. It is a modern cathedral in the old Gothic style, and was built between 1904 and 1978.

Robin Hood 25
Roche Abbey, Maltby 27
Roman Empire 4, 5, 29
Romans 4, 5
Rome 4, 5, 7, 15, 21, 29

saints 7, 11, 14, 15, 17, 18, 19, 20
shrines 15, 17, 18
St Davids 14, 29
St David's Cathedral 14–15
St Martin's Church, Canterbury 6–7
St Mary's Abbey, York 24
stained glass windows 9, 12
Synod of Whitby 21, 29

Thames, River 22
Thirsk, William 27

Vikings 13, 18
villas 4, 5

Westminster Abbey 22–23, 29
Whitby Abbey 20–21
William the Conqueror 22
World War II 28
worship 6, 13

York Minster 29
Yorkshire 5, 20, 27